50 Delicious Strawberry Baked Dishes

By: Kelly Johnson

Table of Contents

- Strawberry Shortcake
- Strawberry Muffins
- Strawberry Cheesecake
- Strawberry Cupcakes
- Strawberry Cake
- Strawberry Pie
- Strawberry Scones
- Strawberry Jam Tarts
- Strawberry Galette
- Strawberry Streusel Bars
- Strawberry Crumble
- Strawberry Focaccia
- Strawberry Brownies
- Strawberry Cobbler
- Strawberry Almond Cake
- Strawberry Rhubarb Pie
- Strawberry Oatmeal Cookies
- Strawberry Danish
- Strawberry Pudding Cake

- Strawberry Bread
- Strawberry Turnovers
- Strawberry Churros
- Strawberry Biscotti
- Strawberry Swirl Cheesecake Bars
- Strawberry Clafoutis
- Strawberry Bundt Cake
- Strawberry Meringue Pie
- Strawberry Cream Cheese Danish
- Strawberry Macarons
- Strawberry Puff Pastry Twists
- Strawberry Layer Cake
- Strawberry Crinkle Cookies
- Strawberry Tiramisu
- Strawberry Sorbet Cake
- Strawberry Blondies
- Strawberry Cake Roll
- Strawberry Tart
- Strawberry and Cream Scones
- Strawberry Pecan Bars
- Strawberry Pancake Bake

- Strawberry Yogurt Cake
- Strawberry Mousse Cake
- Strawberry Lemonade Cake
- Strawberry and White Chocolate Cookies
- Strawberry Swirl Pound Cake
- Strawberry Streusel Muffins
- Strawberry Peach Cobbler
- Strawberry Rice Pudding Cake
- Strawberry Macadamia Cookies
- Strawberry Ice Cream Cake

Strawberry Shortcake

Ingredients:

- 2 cups (250g) all-purpose flour
- 1/4 cup (50g) sugar
- 1 tbsp baking powder
- 1/2 tsp salt
- 1/2 cup (115g) unsalted butter, cold and cubed
- 2/3 cup (160ml) heavy cream
- 1 tsp vanilla extract
- 1 lb (450g) fresh strawberries, sliced
- 1/4 cup (50g) sugar (for strawberries)
- Whipped cream (for serving)

Instructions:

1. Preheat oven to 375°F (190°C). Grease a baking sheet.
2. In a bowl, whisk together flour, sugar, baking powder, and salt.
3. Cut in the butter until the mixture resembles coarse crumbs.
4. Stir in the cream and vanilla extract until just combined.
5. Drop spoonfuls of dough onto the prepared baking sheet and bake for 12-15 minutes, or until golden.
6. Mix strawberries with 1/4 cup sugar and let sit for 10 minutes.
7. Slice the shortcakes in half, top with strawberries and whipped cream, and serve.

Strawberry Muffins

Ingredients:

- 2 cups (250g) all-purpose flour
- 1/2 cup (100g) sugar
- 1 tsp baking powder
- 1/2 tsp baking soda
- 1/4 tsp salt
- 1/2 cup (120ml) milk
- 1/2 cup (115g) unsalted butter, melted
- 1 large egg
- 1 tsp vanilla extract
- 1 1/2 cups (225g) fresh strawberries, chopped

Instructions:

1. Preheat oven to 350°F (175°C). Line a muffin tin with paper liners.
2. In a large bowl, whisk together flour, sugar, baking powder, baking soda, and salt.
3. In another bowl, combine milk, melted butter, egg, and vanilla extract.
4. Stir the wet ingredients into the dry ingredients until just combined.
5. Gently fold in the strawberries.
6. Spoon the batter into muffin cups and bake for 20-25 minutes, or until a toothpick comes out clean.

Strawberry Cheesecake

Ingredients:

- 1 1/2 cups (180g) graham cracker crumbs
- 1/4 cup (50g) sugar
- 1/2 cup (115g) unsalted butter, melted
- 3 cups (675g) cream cheese, softened
- 1 cup (200g) sugar
- 1 tsp vanilla extract
- 3 large eggs
- 1/2 cup (120ml) sour cream
- 2 cups (300g) fresh strawberries, chopped

Instructions:

1. Preheat oven to 325°F (165°C). Grease a 9-inch springform pan.
2. In a bowl, mix graham cracker crumbs, sugar, and melted butter. Press the mixture into the bottom of the pan to form a crust.
3. Beat the cream cheese, sugar, and vanilla extract until smooth. Add the eggs one at a time, mixing well after each addition.
4. Add the sour cream and mix until smooth.
5. Pour the cream cheese mixture into the crust and bake for 50-60 minutes, or until set.
6. Let cool to room temperature, then refrigerate for at least 4 hours.
7. Top with fresh strawberries before serving.

Strawberry Cupcakes

Ingredients:

- 1 1/2 cups (190g) all-purpose flour
- 1 cup (200g) sugar
- 1 1/2 tsp baking powder
- 1/4 tsp salt
- 1/2 cup (120ml) milk
- 1/2 cup (115g) unsalted butter, softened
- 2 large eggs
- 1 tsp vanilla extract
- 1/2 cup (75g) fresh strawberries, chopped

Instructions:

1. Preheat oven to 350°F (175°C). Line a muffin tin with paper liners.
2. In a bowl, whisk together flour, sugar, baking powder, and salt.
3. In another bowl, beat together milk, butter, eggs, and vanilla extract until smooth.
4. Gradually add the dry ingredients to the wet mixture, mixing until just combined.
5. Gently fold in the chopped strawberries.
6. Spoon the batter into muffin cups and bake for 18-20 minutes, or until a toothpick comes out clean.

Strawberry Cake

Ingredients:

- 2 cups (250g) all-purpose flour
- 1 1/2 cups (300g) sugar
- 1 tsp baking powder
- 1/2 tsp baking soda
- 1/4 tsp salt
- 1/2 cup (120ml) milk
- 1/2 cup (115g) unsalted butter, softened
- 2 large eggs
- 1 tsp vanilla extract
- 1 1/2 cups (225g) fresh strawberries, pureed

Instructions:

1. Preheat oven to 350°F (175°C). Grease and flour a 9-inch round cake pan.
2. In a bowl, whisk together flour, sugar, baking powder, baking soda, and salt.
3. In another bowl, beat together milk, butter, eggs, and vanilla extract.
4. Gradually add the dry ingredients to the wet mixture, mixing until smooth.
5. Stir in the pureed strawberries.
6. Pour the batter into the prepared cake pan and bake for 25-30 minutes, or until a toothpick comes out clean.

Strawberry Pie

Ingredients:

- 1 pre-baked pie crust
- 3 cups (450g) fresh strawberries, halved
- 1 cup (200g) sugar
- 2 tbsp cornstarch
- 1/2 cup (120ml) water
- 1 tbsp lemon juice

Instructions:

1. Preheat oven to 375°F (190°C).
2. In a saucepan, combine sugar, cornstarch, and water. Bring to a boil and cook until thickened.
3. Remove from heat and stir in lemon juice. Let cool.
4. Place the halved strawberries in the pre-baked pie crust.
5. Pour the cooled syrup over the strawberries, covering them evenly.
6. Bake for 15-20 minutes, or until the filling is bubbly and set. Let cool before serving.

Strawberry Scones

Ingredients:

- 2 cups (250g) all-purpose flour
- 1/4 cup (50g) sugar
- 1 tbsp baking powder
- 1/4 tsp salt
- 1/2 cup (115g) unsalted butter, cold and cubed
- 1/2 cup (120ml) heavy cream
- 1 large egg
- 1 tsp vanilla extract
- 1 cup (150g) fresh strawberries, chopped

Instructions:

1. Preheat oven to 375°F (190°C). Line a baking sheet with parchment paper.
2. In a bowl, whisk together flour, sugar, baking powder, and salt.
3. Cut in the butter until the mixture resembles coarse crumbs.
4. In another bowl, mix the cream, egg, and vanilla extract.
5. Stir the wet ingredients into the dry mixture and gently fold in the strawberries.
6. Drop spoonfuls of dough onto the baking sheet and bake for 12-15 minutes, or until golden.

Strawberry Jam Tarts

Ingredients:

- 1 sheet puff pastry, thawed
- 1/2 cup (160g) strawberry jam
- 1 egg, beaten (for egg wash)

Instructions:

1. Preheat oven to 375°F (190°C).
2. Roll out the puff pastry and cut into small circles using a cookie cutter.
3. Place the circles into a muffin tin and spoon a small amount of strawberry jam into the center of each.
4. Brush the edges of the pastry with the beaten egg.
5. Bake for 12-15 minutes, or until golden and puffed.

Strawberry Galette

Ingredients:

- 1 sheet pie crust
- 2 cups (300g) fresh strawberries, sliced
- 1/4 cup (50g) sugar
- 1 tbsp cornstarch
- 1 tbsp lemon juice
- 1 egg, beaten (for egg wash)

Instructions:

1. Preheat oven to 375°F (190°C). Line a baking sheet with parchment paper.
2. In a bowl, toss strawberries with sugar, cornstarch, and lemon juice.
3. Roll out the pie crust and place the strawberry mixture in the center.
4. Fold the edges of the crust over the strawberries, leaving the center exposed.
5. Brush the crust with the beaten egg and bake for 30-35 minutes, or until the crust is golden.

Strawberry Streusel Bars

Ingredients:

- 2 cups (250g) all-purpose flour
- 1/2 cup (100g) sugar
- 1 tsp baking powder
- 1/2 tsp salt
- 1/2 cup (115g) unsalted butter, cold and cubed
- 1 large egg
- 1/2 tsp vanilla extract
- 1 cup (150g) fresh strawberries, chopped
- 1/4 cup (50g) sugar (for strawberries)
- 1/2 cup (50g) rolled oats
- 1/4 cup (30g) brown sugar

Instructions:

1. Preheat oven to 350°F (175°C). Grease a 9x9-inch baking pan.
2. In a bowl, combine flour, sugar, baking powder, and salt.
3. Cut in butter until the mixture resembles coarse crumbs.
4. Beat in the egg and vanilla extract.
5. Press 2/3 of the dough into the prepared pan to form the base.
6. Toss the strawberries with sugar and spread over the dough.
7. Sprinkle the remaining dough over the strawberries, followed by the oats and brown sugar.

8. Bake for 30-35 minutes, or until golden and set.

Strawberry Crumble

Ingredients:

- 3 cups (450g) fresh strawberries, sliced
- 1/4 cup (50g) sugar
- 1 tbsp cornstarch
- 1 tbsp lemon juice
- 1 cup (125g) all-purpose flour
- 1/2 cup (100g) sugar
- 1/2 cup (115g) unsalted butter, cold and cubed
- 1/2 cup (50g) rolled oats

Instructions:

1. Preheat oven to 375°F (190°C). Grease a baking dish.
2. In a bowl, toss the strawberries with sugar, cornstarch, and lemon juice.
3. In a separate bowl, combine flour, sugar, and butter, mixing until it resembles coarse crumbs.
4. Stir in the oats.
5. Pour the strawberry mixture into the prepared dish and sprinkle the crumble mixture over the top.
6. Bake for 25-30 minutes, or until golden and bubbling.

Strawberry Focaccia

Ingredients:

- 1 lb (450g) pizza dough
- 1 cup (150g) fresh strawberries, halved
- 1 tbsp olive oil
- 1 tbsp sugar
- Sea salt for topping

Instructions:

1. Preheat oven to 400°F (200°C).
2. Roll the pizza dough out into a rectangle on a baking sheet.
3. Arrange the strawberry halves on top of the dough.
4. Drizzle with olive oil and sprinkle with sugar.
5. Bake for 20-25 minutes, or until golden and cooked through.
6. Sprinkle with sea salt before serving.

Strawberry Brownies

Ingredients:

- 1/2 cup (115g) unsalted butter, melted
- 1 cup (200g) sugar
- 2 large eggs
- 1 tsp vanilla extract
- 1 cup (125g) all-purpose flour
- 1/4 cup (30g) cocoa powder
- 1/4 tsp salt
- 1 cup (150g) fresh strawberries, chopped

Instructions:

1. Preheat oven to 350°F (175°C). Grease a baking pan.
2. In a bowl, whisk together melted butter, sugar, eggs, and vanilla extract.
3. In another bowl, mix together flour, cocoa powder, and salt.
4. Gradually add the dry ingredients to the wet ingredients.
5. Fold in the chopped strawberries.
6. Pour the batter into the prepared pan and bake for 20-25 minutes, or until a toothpick comes out clean.

Strawberry Cobbler

Ingredients:

- 4 cups (600g) fresh strawberries, hulled and sliced
- 1/4 cup (50g) sugar
- 1 tbsp lemon juice
- 1 tsp vanilla extract
- 1 cup (125g) all-purpose flour
- 1/4 cup (50g) sugar
- 1/4 tsp salt
- 1 tsp baking powder
- 1/2 tsp baking soda
- 1/2 cup (115g) unsalted butter, cubed
- 1/2 cup (120ml) heavy cream

Instructions:

1. Preheat oven to 375°F (190°C). Grease a baking dish.
2. In a bowl, toss strawberries with sugar, lemon juice, and vanilla extract.
3. In a separate bowl, whisk together flour, sugar, salt, baking powder, and baking soda.
4. Cut in the butter until the mixture resembles coarse crumbs.
5. Stir in the heavy cream until a dough forms.
6. Spoon the dough over the strawberries in the prepared dish.
7. Bake for 35-40 minutes, or until the topping is golden and the filling is bubbly.

Strawberry Almond Cake

Ingredients:

- 1 cup (125g) all-purpose flour
- 1/2 cup (50g) almond flour
- 1 tsp baking powder
- 1/4 tsp salt
- 1/2 cup (115g) unsalted butter, softened
- 1 cup (200g) sugar
- 2 large eggs
- 1 tsp vanilla extract
- 1/2 cup (120ml) milk
- 1 cup (150g) fresh strawberries, sliced

Instructions:

1. Preheat oven to 350°F (175°C). Grease a cake pan.
2. In a bowl, combine flour, almond flour, baking powder, and salt.
3. In another bowl, beat butter and sugar together until fluffy.
4. Add the eggs, one at a time, followed by vanilla extract.
5. Gradually mix in the dry ingredients and milk.
6. Fold in the sliced strawberries.
7. Pour the batter into the pan and bake for 30-35 minutes, or until golden and a toothpick comes out clean.

Strawberry Rhubarb Pie

Ingredients:

- 2 cups (300g) fresh strawberries, hulled and sliced
- 2 cups (300g) rhubarb, chopped
- 1 1/2 cups (300g) sugar
- 1/4 cup (30g) cornstarch
- 1 tbsp lemon juice
- 1/2 tsp vanilla extract
- 1 pie crust, pre-baked or fresh
- 1 egg, beaten (for egg wash)

Instructions:

1. Preheat oven to 375°F (190°C).
2. In a bowl, combine strawberries, rhubarb, sugar, cornstarch, lemon juice, and vanilla extract.
3. Pour the filling into the pie crust.
4. Cover with the top pie crust and seal the edges.
5. Brush with the beaten egg.
6. Bake for 45-50 minutes, or until the crust is golden and the filling is bubbling.

Strawberry Oatmeal Cookies

Ingredients:

- 1 cup (125g) all-purpose flour
- 1/2 cup (50g) rolled oats
- 1/2 tsp baking soda
- 1/4 tsp salt
- 1/2 cup (115g) unsalted butter, softened
- 1/2 cup (100g) sugar
- 1/4 cup (50g) brown sugar
- 1 large egg
- 1 tsp vanilla extract
- 1 cup (150g) fresh strawberries, chopped

Instructions:

1. Preheat oven to 350°F (175°C). Line a baking sheet with parchment paper.
2. In a bowl, combine flour, oats, baking soda, and salt.
3. In another bowl, beat butter, sugar, and brown sugar until creamy.
4. Add the egg and vanilla extract and beat until smooth.
5. Gradually add the dry ingredients and mix until combined.
6. Fold in the chopped strawberries.
7. Drop spoonfuls of dough onto the baking sheet and bake for 12-15 minutes, or until golden.

Strawberry Danish

Ingredients:

- 1 sheet puff pastry, thawed
- 1/2 cup (120g) cream cheese, softened
- 1/4 cup (50g) sugar
- 1 tsp vanilla extract
- 1 cup (150g) fresh strawberries, chopped
- 1 egg, beaten (for egg wash)

Instructions:

1. Preheat oven to 375°F (190°C).
2. Roll out the puff pastry and cut into squares.
3. In a bowl, mix cream cheese, sugar, and vanilla extract.
4. Spoon the cream cheese mixture onto the center of each puff pastry square.
5. Top with chopped strawberries and fold the edges to form a rectangle.
6. Brush with the beaten egg.
7. Bake for 15-20 minutes, or until golden and puffed.

Strawberry Pudding Cake

Ingredients:

- 1 cup (150g) fresh strawberries, chopped
- 1/2 cup (100g) sugar
- 2 tbsp lemon juice
- 1 cup (125g) all-purpose flour
- 1 tsp baking powder
- 1/4 tsp salt
- 1/2 cup (115g) unsalted butter, melted
- 1/2 cup (120ml) milk
- 1 large egg
- 1 tsp vanilla extract
- 1/4 cup (50g) sugar (for topping)

Instructions:

1. Preheat oven to 350°F (175°C). Grease a baking dish.
2. In a bowl, combine strawberries with sugar and lemon juice, and let sit for 10 minutes.
3. In another bowl, whisk together flour, baking powder, salt, melted butter, milk, egg, and vanilla.
4. Pour the batter into the prepared dish, then spoon the strawberry mixture on top.
5. Sprinkle sugar over the top and bake for 35-40 minutes, until golden and set.

Strawberry Bread

Ingredients:

- 2 cups (250g) all-purpose flour
- 1 tsp baking soda
- 1/2 tsp salt
- 1/2 cup (115g) unsalted butter, softened
- 1 cup (200g) sugar
- 2 large eggs
- 1 tsp vanilla extract
- 1 cup (150g) fresh strawberries, chopped
- 1/2 cup (120ml) milk

Instructions:

1. Preheat oven to 350°F (175°C). Grease a loaf pan.
2. In a bowl, combine flour, baking soda, and salt.
3. In another bowl, beat butter and sugar until creamy.
4. Add eggs, one at a time, then stir in vanilla extract.
5. Gradually add the dry ingredients and milk, mixing until smooth.
6. Fold in chopped strawberries.
7. Pour the batter into the prepared pan and bake for 55-60 minutes, or until a toothpick comes out clean.

Strawberry Turnovers

Ingredients:

- 1 sheet puff pastry, thawed
- 1 cup (150g) fresh strawberries, chopped
- 1/4 cup (50g) sugar
- 1 tbsp cornstarch
- 1 tsp lemon juice
- 1 egg, beaten (for egg wash)

Instructions:

1. Preheat oven to 375°F (190°C).
2. Roll out puff pastry and cut into squares.
3. In a bowl, mix strawberries, sugar, cornstarch, and lemon juice.
4. Spoon the strawberry mixture onto the center of each square.
5. Fold the pastry over the filling to form a triangle.
6. Press the edges to seal and brush with egg wash.
7. Bake for 20-25 minutes, or until golden brown.

Strawberry Churros

Ingredients:

- 1 cup (120g) all-purpose flour
- 1 tbsp sugar
- 1/4 tsp salt
- 1/2 cup (120ml) water
- 1/4 cup (55g) unsalted butter
- 1 tsp vanilla extract
- 1/4 tsp ground cinnamon
- 1/2 cup (120g) fresh strawberries, chopped
- Oil for frying
- Sugar for coating

Instructions:

1. In a saucepan, combine water, butter, and sugar. Bring to a boil.
2. Remove from heat and stir in flour and salt until combined.
3. Allow the mixture to cool slightly, then mix in the vanilla extract.
4. Transfer to a piping bag with a star tip.
5. Heat oil in a frying pan to 375°F (190°C).
6. Pipe strips of dough into the hot oil and fry until golden brown.
7. Drain on paper towels and toss in sugar and cinnamon.
8. Mix chopped strawberries into a simple glaze and drizzle over the churros.

Strawberry Biscotti

Ingredients:

- 2 cups (250g) all-purpose flour
- 1 tsp baking powder
- 1/2 tsp salt
- 1/2 cup (100g) sugar
- 1/2 cup (115g) unsalted butter, softened
- 2 large eggs
- 1 tsp vanilla extract
- 1 cup (150g) fresh strawberries, chopped
- 1/2 cup (60g) almonds, chopped

Instructions:

1. Preheat oven to 350°F (175°C). Line a baking sheet with parchment paper.
2. In a bowl, whisk together flour, baking powder, and salt.
3. In another bowl, beat butter and sugar until creamy.
4. Add eggs, one at a time, and vanilla extract.
5. Gradually mix in the dry ingredients, followed by strawberries and almonds.
6. Shape the dough into a log and place on the baking sheet.
7. Bake for 25-30 minutes, then remove and cool slightly.
8. Slice the log into biscotti pieces and bake for an additional 10-15 minutes until crisp.

Strawberry Swirl Cheesecake Bars

Ingredients:

- 1 1/2 cups (150g) graham cracker crumbs
- 1/4 cup (50g) sugar
- 1/2 cup (115g) unsalted butter, melted
- 2 cups (450g) cream cheese, softened
- 1/2 cup (100g) sugar
- 1 tsp vanilla extract
- 2 large eggs
- 1 cup (150g) fresh strawberries, pureed

Instructions:

1. Preheat oven to 325°F (165°C). Grease a baking pan.
2. In a bowl, combine graham cracker crumbs, sugar, and melted butter. Press into the bottom of the pan to form the crust.
3. In another bowl, beat cream cheese and sugar until smooth. Add eggs and vanilla extract.
4. Pour the cream cheese mixture over the crust.
5. Swirl pureed strawberries into the cream cheese mixture.
6. Bake for 30-35 minutes, or until set. Cool completely and refrigerate for at least 2 hours before cutting into bars.

Strawberry Clafoutis

Ingredients:

- 2 cups (300g) fresh strawberries, halved
- 1 cup (125g) all-purpose flour
- 1/2 cup (100g) sugar
- 1/2 tsp vanilla extract
- 1 1/2 cups (360ml) milk
- 3 large eggs
- 1/4 tsp salt

Instructions:

1. Preheat oven to 350°F (175°C). Grease a baking dish.
2. Arrange the strawberries in the bottom of the dish.
3. In a bowl, whisk together flour, sugar, vanilla, milk, eggs, and salt until smooth.
4. Pour the batter over the strawberries.
5. Bake for 35-40 minutes, or until golden and puffed.

Strawberry Bundt Cake

Ingredients:

- 2 cups (250g) all-purpose flour
- 1 tsp baking powder
- 1/2 tsp salt
- 1/2 cup (115g) unsalted butter, softened
- 1 cup (200g) sugar
- 2 large eggs
- 1 tsp vanilla extract
- 1/2 cup (120ml) milk
- 1 cup (150g) fresh strawberries, chopped

Instructions:

1. Preheat oven to 350°F (175°C). Grease a Bundt pan.
2. In a bowl, whisk together flour, baking powder, and salt.
3. In another bowl, beat butter and sugar until creamy.
4. Add eggs, one at a time, and vanilla extract.
5. Gradually mix in the dry ingredients and milk, followed by chopped strawberries.
6. Pour the batter into the pan and bake for 45-50 minutes, or until a toothpick comes out clean.

Strawberry Meringue Pie

Ingredients:

- 1 pie crust, pre-baked
- 1 cup (150g) fresh strawberries, pureed
- 1/4 cup (50g) sugar
- 1 tbsp cornstarch
- 2 large egg whites
- 1/2 tsp vanilla extract
- 1/4 tsp cream of tartar

Instructions:

1. Preheat oven to 350°F (175°C).
2. In a saucepan, combine strawberry puree, sugar, and cornstarch. Cook over medium heat until thickened.
3. Remove from heat and let cool.
4. Beat egg whites, vanilla extract, and cream of tartar until stiff peaks form.
5. Spread the strawberry mixture into the pie crust and top with meringue.
6. Bake for 15-20 minutes, or until the meringue is golden.

Strawberry Cream Cheese Danish

Ingredients:

- 1 sheet puff pastry, thawed
- 4 oz (115g) cream cheese, softened
- 1/4 cup (50g) sugar
- 1 tsp vanilla extract
- 1 cup (150g) fresh strawberries, chopped
- 1 egg, beaten (for egg wash)

Instructions:

1. Preheat oven to 375°F (190°C).
2. Roll out puff pastry and cut into squares.
3. In a bowl, mix cream cheese, sugar, and vanilla extract.
4. Spoon the cream cheese mixture onto the center of each pastry square.
5. Top with chopped strawberries and fold the pastry over.
6. Brush with egg wash and bake for 15-20 minutes, until golden and puffed.

Strawberry Macarons

Ingredients:

- 1 cup (100g) powdered sugar
- 1/2 cup (50g) almond flour
- 2 large egg whites
- 1/4 cup (50g) granulated sugar
- 1/2 tsp vanilla extract
- 1/4 cup (60g) fresh strawberries, pureed
- 1/2 cup (120g) unsalted butter, softened
- 1 cup (120g) powdered sugar (for filling)

Instructions:

1. Preheat oven to 300°F (150°C). Line a baking sheet with parchment paper.
2. Sift together powdered sugar and almond flour.
3. In a separate bowl, beat egg whites until stiff peaks form. Gradually add granulated sugar while beating.
4. Gently fold the sifted dry ingredients into the egg whites.
5. Pipe small rounds of batter onto the prepared sheet. Tap the sheet to remove air bubbles.
6. Let the macarons sit for 20-30 minutes until they form a skin.
7. Bake for 15-20 minutes, then cool completely.
8. To make the filling, whip butter and powdered sugar together until smooth, then fold in the strawberry puree.
9. Pair up the macaron shells and fill with the strawberry buttercream.

Strawberry Puff Pastry Twists

Ingredients:

- 1 sheet puff pastry, thawed
- 1/2 cup (120g) strawberry jam
- 1 tbsp sugar
- 1 egg, beaten (for egg wash)

Instructions:

1. Preheat oven to 375°F (190°C).
2. Roll out puff pastry and spread strawberry jam evenly on top.
3. Sprinkle with sugar.
4. Cut the pastry into strips and twist each strip.
5. Place on a baking sheet and brush with egg wash.
6. Bake for 15-20 minutes, or until golden brown and flaky.

Strawberry Layer Cake

Ingredients:

- 2 cups (250g) all-purpose flour
- 1 1/2 tsp baking powder
- 1/2 tsp salt
- 1/2 cup (115g) unsalted butter, softened
- 1 cup (200g) sugar
- 2 large eggs
- 1 tsp vanilla extract
- 1/2 cup (120ml) milk
- 1 cup (150g) fresh strawberries, chopped

For Frosting:

- 1/2 cup (115g) unsalted butter, softened
- 2 cups (250g) powdered sugar
- 1/4 cup (60g) strawberry puree
- 1 tsp vanilla extract

Instructions:

1. Preheat oven to 350°F (175°C). Grease two 8-inch round cake pans.
2. In a bowl, whisk together flour, baking powder, and salt.
3. In another bowl, beat butter and sugar until creamy. Add eggs and vanilla, then mix in the dry ingredients and milk.

4. Fold in chopped strawberries.

5. Divide the batter between the prepared pans and bake for 25-30 minutes. Let the cakes cool completely.

6. For the frosting, beat butter and powdered sugar until smooth, then add strawberry puree and vanilla.

7. Frost the cooled cakes and layer them, garnishing with extra strawberries if desired.

Strawberry Crinkle Cookies

Ingredients:

- 1 1/2 cups (190g) all-purpose flour
- 1/2 tsp baking powder
- 1/4 tsp salt
- 1/2 cup (115g) unsalted butter, softened
- 1 cup (200g) sugar
- 2 large eggs
- 1/2 cup (120g) fresh strawberries, pureed
- 1/4 cup (50g) powdered sugar

Instructions:

1. Preheat oven to 350°F (175°C). Line a baking sheet with parchment paper.
2. In a bowl, whisk together flour, baking powder, and salt.
3. In another bowl, beat butter and sugar until light and fluffy. Add eggs and strawberry puree.
4. Gradually mix in the dry ingredients.
5. Roll dough into balls and coat with powdered sugar.
6. Place on the prepared baking sheet and bake for 10-12 minutes, until the edges are golden.

Strawberry Tiramisu

Ingredients:

- 1 pint (300g) fresh strawberries, sliced
- 1 package (7 oz) ladyfingers
- 1 cup (240ml) heavy cream
- 1/2 cup (100g) sugar
- 8 oz (225g) mascarpone cheese
- 1 tsp vanilla extract
- 1/4 cup (60ml) strawberry liqueur (optional)

Instructions:

1. In a bowl, whip the cream and sugar until stiff peaks form.
2. In another bowl, whisk mascarpone cheese and vanilla extract until smooth.
3. Gently fold the whipped cream into the mascarpone mixture.
4. Dip ladyfingers in strawberry liqueur (if using) or water, then layer them in the bottom of a dish.
5. Spread half of the mascarpone mixture over the ladyfingers. Top with half of the sliced strawberries.
6. Repeat the layers and refrigerate for at least 4 hours before serving.

Strawberry Sorbet Cake

Ingredients:

- 1 pint (300g) fresh strawberries, pureed
- 1/2 cup (100g) sugar
- 1 tbsp lemon juice
- 2 cups (480ml) heavy cream
- 1/2 cup (100g) sugar
- 1/2 tsp vanilla extract

Instructions:

1. In a bowl, combine strawberry puree, sugar, and lemon juice. Mix well and freeze in a shallow pan for 3-4 hours, scraping with a fork every 30 minutes to create sorbet.
2. In a separate bowl, whip cream, sugar, and vanilla until stiff peaks form.
3. In a cake pan, layer the whipped cream and sorbet alternately.
4. Freeze the cake for at least 4 hours, or until firm.

Strawberry Blondies

Ingredients:

- 1 cup (125g) all-purpose flour
- 1/2 tsp baking powder
- 1/4 tsp salt
- 1/2 cup (115g) unsalted butter, melted
- 1 cup (200g) brown sugar
- 1 large egg
- 1 tsp vanilla extract
- 1/2 cup (75g) fresh strawberries, chopped

Instructions:

1. Preheat oven to 350°F (175°C). Grease an 8x8-inch baking pan.
2. In a bowl, whisk together flour, baking powder, and salt.
3. In another bowl, mix melted butter and brown sugar until smooth. Add egg and vanilla, then stir in the dry ingredients.
4. Fold in chopped strawberries.
5. Pour the batter into the prepared pan and bake for 25-30 minutes. Let cool before slicing into squares.

Strawberry Cake Roll

Ingredients:

- 1 cup (125g) all-purpose flour
- 1 tsp baking powder
- 1/4 tsp salt
- 1/2 cup (115g) unsalted butter, softened
- 1 cup (200g) sugar
- 4 large eggs
- 1 tsp vanilla extract
- 1 cup (150g) fresh strawberries, pureed

For Frosting:

- 8 oz (225g) cream cheese, softened
- 1/2 cup (115g) unsalted butter, softened
- 2 cups (250g) powdered sugar
- 1 tsp vanilla extract

Instructions:

1. Preheat oven to 350°F (175°C). Grease a jelly roll pan and line with parchment paper.
2. In a bowl, whisk together flour, baking powder, and salt.
3. In another bowl, beat butter and sugar until creamy. Add eggs and vanilla, then fold in the dry ingredients and strawberry puree.
4. Pour the batter into the prepared pan and bake for 15-18 minutes.

5. Cool the cake, then roll it up with a towel to prevent cracking.

6. For the frosting, beat cream cheese and butter until smooth, then mix in powdered sugar and vanilla.

7. Unroll the cooled cake and frost, then roll it back up.

Strawberry Tart

Ingredients:

- 1 premade tart shell
- 1 pint (300g) fresh strawberries, sliced
- 1/2 cup (100g) sugar
- 1 tbsp cornstarch
- 1/2 tsp lemon juice
- 1/4 cup (60ml) water

Instructions:

1. Preheat oven to 350°F (175°C). Bake the tart shell according to package instructions.
2. In a saucepan, combine sugar, cornstarch, lemon juice, and water. Bring to a boil until thickened.
3. Stir in sliced strawberries and cook for another 2-3 minutes.
4. Pour the mixture into the baked tart shell and refrigerate for at least 2 hours before serving.

Strawberry and Cream Scones

Ingredients:

- 2 cups (250g) all-purpose flour
- 1/4 cup (50g) sugar
- 2 tsp baking powder
- 1/4 tsp salt
- 1/2 cup (115g) unsalted butter, cold and cubed
- 1/2 cup (120ml) heavy cream
- 1 cup (150g) fresh strawberries, chopped

Instructions:

1. Preheat oven to 375°F (190°C). Line a baking sheet with parchment paper.
2. In a bowl, whisk together flour, sugar, baking powder, and salt.
3. Cut in the cold butter until the mixture resembles coarse crumbs.
4. Stir in heavy cream and fold in chopped strawberries.
5. Turn the dough onto a floured surface and shape into a circle. Cut into wedges.
6. Place on the baking sheet and bake for 15-20 minutes, until golden.

Strawberry Pecan Bars

Ingredients:

- 1 1/2 cups (190g) all-purpose flour
- 1/2 cup (115g) unsalted butter, softened
- 1/4 cup (50g) granulated sugar
- 1/2 cup (60g) chopped pecans
- 1/4 tsp salt
- 1 cup (150g) fresh strawberries, chopped
- 1/4 cup (50g) powdered sugar

Instructions:

1. Preheat oven to 350°F (175°C). Grease an 8x8-inch baking pan.
2. In a bowl, mix together flour, butter, sugar, and salt until a dough forms.
3. Press the dough into the prepared pan and bake for 15 minutes.
4. In another bowl, combine chopped strawberries and pecans.
5. Spread the strawberry-pecan mixture over the crust and bake for an additional 25 minutes.
6. Let cool and dust with powdered sugar before slicing into bars.

Strawberry Pancake Bake

Ingredients:

- 2 cups (250g) all-purpose flour
- 2 tbsp sugar
- 2 tsp baking powder
- 1/2 tsp salt
- 2 large eggs
- 1 cup (240ml) milk
- 1/2 cup (115g) unsalted butter, melted
- 1 tsp vanilla extract
- 1 1/2 cups (200g) fresh strawberries, sliced

Instructions:

1. Preheat oven to 375°F (190°C). Grease a 9x9-inch baking dish.
2. In a bowl, whisk together flour, sugar, baking powder, and salt.
3. In another bowl, beat eggs, milk, melted butter, and vanilla extract.
4. Pour the wet ingredients into the dry ingredients and mix until combined.
5. Fold in the sliced strawberries.
6. Pour the batter into the prepared dish and bake for 30-35 minutes. Serve with maple syrup.

Strawberry Yogurt Cake

Ingredients:

- 1 cup (125g) all-purpose flour
- 1/2 tsp baking powder
- 1/4 tsp baking soda
- 1/4 tsp salt
- 1/2 cup (120g) unsalted butter, softened
- 1 cup (200g) sugar
- 2 large eggs
- 1/2 cup (120g) plain yogurt
- 1 tsp vanilla extract
- 1 cup (150g) fresh strawberries, chopped

Instructions:

1. Preheat oven to 350°F (175°C). Grease a 9-inch round cake pan.
2. In a bowl, whisk together flour, baking powder, baking soda, and salt.
3. In another bowl, beat butter and sugar until light and fluffy. Add eggs one at a time.
4. Mix in the yogurt and vanilla extract. Gradually add the dry ingredients and mix until smooth.
5. Fold in chopped strawberries.
6. Pour the batter into the pan and bake for 25-30 minutes or until a toothpick comes out clean. Let cool before serving.

Strawberry Mousse Cake

Ingredients:

- 1 1/2 cups (190g) graham cracker crumbs
- 1/4 cup (50g) sugar
- 1/2 cup (115g) unsalted butter, melted
- 2 cups (300g) fresh strawberries, pureed
- 1/2 cup (100g) sugar
- 2 cups (480ml) heavy cream
- 2 tsp gelatin powder
- 2 tbsp cold water
- 1 tsp vanilla extract

Instructions:

1. Preheat oven to 350°F (175°C). Grease a 9-inch springform pan.
2. In a bowl, combine graham cracker crumbs, sugar, and melted butter. Press into the bottom of the pan and bake for 10 minutes. Let cool.
3. In a small bowl, sprinkle gelatin over cold water and let bloom for 5 minutes.
4. In a saucepan, heat pureed strawberries and sugar until the sugar dissolves. Add the gelatin mixture and stir until dissolved. Remove from heat and let cool.
5. In a large bowl, whip heavy cream until stiff peaks form. Gently fold in the strawberry mixture and vanilla extract.
6. Pour the mousse over the crust and refrigerate for at least 4 hours or overnight before serving.

Strawberry Lemonade Cake

Ingredients:

- 2 cups (250g) all-purpose flour
- 1 1/2 tsp baking powder
- 1/4 tsp salt
- 1/2 cup (115g) unsalted butter, softened
- 1 cup (200g) sugar
- 2 large eggs
- 1/2 cup (120ml) lemon juice
- 1/2 cup (120g) fresh strawberries, pureed
- 1/4 cup (60ml) milk

Instructions:

1. Preheat oven to 350°F (175°C). Grease a 9-inch round cake pan.
2. In a bowl, whisk together flour, baking powder, and salt.
3. In another bowl, beat butter and sugar until creamy. Add eggs one at a time.
4. Mix in lemon juice, pureed strawberries, and milk. Gradually add the dry ingredients and mix until smooth.
5. Pour the batter into the pan and bake for 25-30 minutes or until a toothpick comes out clean. Let cool.

Strawberry and White Chocolate Cookies

Ingredients:

- 1 1/2 cups (190g) all-purpose flour
- 1/2 tsp baking soda
- 1/4 tsp salt
- 1/2 cup (115g) unsalted butter, softened
- 1 cup (200g) sugar
- 1 large egg
- 1 tsp vanilla extract
- 1 cup (150g) fresh strawberries, chopped
- 1/2 cup (90g) white chocolate chips

Instructions:

1. Preheat oven to 350°F (175°C). Line a baking sheet with parchment paper.
2. In a bowl, whisk together flour, baking soda, and salt.
3. In another bowl, beat butter and sugar until light and fluffy. Add egg and vanilla extract.
4. Gradually add the dry ingredients and mix until combined.
5. Gently fold in the chopped strawberries and white chocolate chips.
6. Drop tablespoonfuls of dough onto the prepared baking sheet and bake for 10-12 minutes, or until golden. Let cool before serving.

Strawberry Swirl Pound Cake

Ingredients:

- 2 1/2 cups (315g) all-purpose flour
- 1 1/2 tsp baking powder
- 1/4 tsp salt
- 1 cup (230g) unsalted butter, softened
- 2 cups (400g) sugar
- 4 large eggs
- 1 tsp vanilla extract
- 1/2 cup (120ml) sour cream
- 1 cup (150g) fresh strawberries, pureed

Instructions:

1. Preheat oven to 350°F (175°C). Grease a 9x5-inch loaf pan.
2. In a bowl, whisk together flour, baking powder, and salt.
3. In another bowl, beat butter and sugar until creamy. Add eggs one at a time, mixing well.
4. Mix in vanilla extract and sour cream. Gradually add the dry ingredients and mix until smooth.
5. Gently fold in the strawberry puree.
6. Pour half of the batter into the prepared pan, then spoon in some strawberry puree and swirl with a knife. Add the remaining batter and swirl again.
7. Bake for 60-70 minutes or until a toothpick comes out clean. Let cool before serving.

Strawberry Streusel Muffins

Ingredients:

- 1 1/2 cups (190g) all-purpose flour
- 1/2 cup (100g) sugar
- 1 tsp baking powder
- 1/2 tsp baking soda
- 1/4 tsp salt
- 1/2 tsp ground cinnamon
- 1/4 cup (60g) unsalted butter, melted
- 1 large egg
- 1/2 cup (120ml) milk
- 1 tsp vanilla extract
- 1 1/2 cups (225g) fresh strawberries, chopped

For the Streusel:

- 1/4 cup (30g) all-purpose flour
- 2 tbsp sugar
- 2 tbsp unsalted butter, cold and cubed
- 1/4 tsp ground cinnamon

Instructions:

1. Preheat oven to 375°F (190°C). Grease a muffin tin or line with paper liners.
2. In a large bowl, mix flour, sugar, baking powder, baking soda, salt, and cinnamon.

3. In a separate bowl, whisk together melted butter, egg, milk, and vanilla extract.

4. Add the wet ingredients to the dry ingredients and mix until just combined. Gently fold in the chopped strawberries.

5. For the streusel, combine flour, sugar, butter, and cinnamon in a small bowl. Use a fork or your fingers to create a crumbly mixture.

6. Spoon the muffin batter into the prepared tin, then top with the streusel mixture.

7. Bake for 18-20 minutes or until a toothpick comes out clean. Let cool before serving.

Strawberry Peach Cobbler

Ingredients:

- 2 cups (300g) fresh strawberries, hulled and sliced
- 2 cups (300g) fresh peaches, peeled and sliced
- 1/4 cup (50g) granulated sugar
- 1 tbsp cornstarch
- 1 tsp lemon juice
- 1/2 tsp vanilla extract

For the Topping:

- 1 cup (125g) all-purpose flour
- 1/4 cup (50g) sugar
- 1 tsp baking powder
- 1/4 tsp salt
- 1/4 cup (60g) unsalted butter, cubed
- 1/4 cup (60ml) milk

Instructions:

1. Preheat oven to 375°F (190°C). Grease a 9x9-inch baking dish.
2. In a bowl, combine strawberries, peaches, sugar, cornstarch, lemon juice, and vanilla extract. Pour the mixture into the prepared dish.
3. In another bowl, whisk together flour, sugar, baking powder, and salt.
4. Cut in the butter until the mixture resembles coarse crumbs. Add the milk and stir until just combined.

5. Spoon the topping over the fruit mixture.

6. Bake for 30-35 minutes or until the topping is golden and the fruit is bubbling. Let cool slightly before serving.

Strawberry Rice Pudding Cake

Ingredients:

- 1 cup (200g) uncooked white rice
- 4 cups (960ml) whole milk
- 1/2 cup (100g) sugar
- 1 tsp vanilla extract
- 1/4 tsp salt
- 1 1/2 cups (225g) fresh strawberries, chopped
- 2 tbsp unsalted butter, melted

Instructions:

1. Preheat oven to 350°F (175°C). Grease a 9-inch round cake pan.
2. In a large saucepan, combine rice, milk, sugar, vanilla extract, and salt. Bring to a simmer over medium heat, stirring frequently.
3. Once the rice is cooked and the mixture has thickened, remove from heat and fold in the chopped strawberries and melted butter.
4. Pour the mixture into the prepared pan and bake for 40-45 minutes, or until the top is golden. Let cool before serving.

Strawberry Macadamia Cookies

Ingredients:

- 1 1/2 cups (190g) all-purpose flour
- 1/2 tsp baking soda
- 1/4 tsp salt
- 1/2 cup (115g) unsalted butter, softened
- 1/2 cup (100g) sugar
- 1/2 cup (100g) packed brown sugar
- 1 large egg
- 1 tsp vanilla extract
- 1 cup (150g) fresh strawberries, chopped
- 1/2 cup (70g) macadamia nuts, chopped

Instructions:

1. Preheat oven to 350°F (175°C). Line a baking sheet with parchment paper.
2. In a bowl, whisk together flour, baking soda, and salt.
3. In another bowl, beat butter, sugar, and brown sugar until creamy. Add egg and vanilla extract.
4. Gradually add the dry ingredients and mix until combined.
5. Gently fold in the chopped strawberries and macadamia nuts.
6. Drop tablespoonfuls of dough onto the prepared baking sheet.
7. Bake for 10-12 minutes, or until golden. Let cool before serving.

Strawberry Ice Cream Cake

Ingredients:

- 1 package (10 oz) graham crackers, crushed
- 1/4 cup (50g) sugar
- 1/2 cup (115g) unsalted butter, melted
- 2 cups (480ml) vanilla ice cream, softened
- 2 cups (300g) fresh strawberries, chopped
- 1/4 cup (50g) sugar

Instructions:

1. Preheat oven to 350°F (175°C). Grease a 9-inch round cake pan.
2. In a bowl, combine crushed graham crackers, sugar, and melted butter. Press the mixture into the bottom of the prepared pan to form a crust. Bake for 10 minutes. Let cool.
3. In a small bowl, mix chopped strawberries with sugar. Let sit for 10 minutes.
4. Layer softened vanilla ice cream on top of the cooled crust. Spoon the strawberries over the ice cream.
5. Freeze for at least 4 hours, or until set. Slice and serve chilled.

www.ingramcontent.com/pod-product-compliance
Lightning Source LLC
LaVergne TN
LVHW081320060526
838201LV00055B/2387